Should Everyone Drive
ELECTRIC CARS?

By Joyce Jeffries

KidHaven
PUBLISHING

Published in 2024 by
KidHaven Publishing, an Imprint of Greenhaven Publishing, LLC
2544 Clinton St.
Buffalo, NY 14224

Designer: Deanna Paternostro
Editor: Katie Kawa

Photo credits: Cover Yeongsik Im/Shutterstock.com; p. 5 (main) Dogora Sun/Shutterstock.com; p. 5 (inset) Noodleki/Wikimedia Commons; p. 7 (top) jittawit21/Shutterstock.com; p. 7 (bottom) Travelpixs/Shutterstock.com; p. 9 (main) VectorMine/Shutterstock.om; p. 9 (inset) Ody_Stocker/ Shutterstock.com; p. 11 Cast Of Thousands/Shutterstock.com; p. 13 Thomas Holt/ Shutterstock.com; p. 15 sungsu han/Shutterstock.com; p. 17 Aleksandr Lupin/Shutterstock.com; p. 19 (main) LightField Studios/Shutterstock.com; p. 19 (inset) Frontpage/Shutterstock.com; p. 21 (notepad) ESB Professional/Shutterstock.com; p. 21 (markers) Kucher Serhii/Shutterstock.com; p. 21 (photo frame) FARBAI/iStock/Thinkstock; p. 21 (inset, left) New Africa/Shutterstock.com; p. 21 (inset, middle) barteverett/Shutterstock.com; p. 21 (inset, right) BigPixel Photo/Shutterstock.com.

Library of Congress Cataloging-in-Publication Data

Names: Jeffries, Joyce, author.
Title: Should everyone drive electric cars? / Joyce Jeffries.
Description: Buffalo, New York : KidHaven Publishing, [2024] | Series:
    Points of view | Includes bibliographical references and index.
Identifiers: LCCN 2023001885 | ISBN 9781534545106 (library binding) | ISBN
    9781534545090 (paperback) | ISBN 9781534545113 (ebook)
Subjects: LCSH: Electric automobiles–Juvenile literature. |
    Automobiles–Environmental aspects–Juvenile literature. | CYAC:
    Electric automobiles. | Automobiles.
Classification: LCC TL220 .J44 2024 | DDC 629.22/93–dc23/eng/20230208
LC record available at https://lccn.loc.gov/2023001885

Printed in the United States of America

Some of the images in this book illustrate individuals who are models. The depictions do not imply actual situations or events.

CPSIA compliance information: Batch #CSKH24: For further information contact Greenhaven Publishing LLC at 1-844-317-7404.

Please visit our website, www.greenhavenpublishing.com. For a free color catalog of all our high-quality books, call toll free 1-844-317-7404 or fax 1-844-317-7405.

Find us on

CONTENTS

A Driving
DEBATE

Cars are one of the most common ways people get around. Some cars run on gasoline, while others run on electricity. Electric cars are becoming more popular. Many people believe they're one of the keys to fighting climate change!

Because electric cars seem to be less harmful for the environment, or natural world, some people argue that they're the only cars that should be on the road. However, other people argue that having the freedom to choose what kind of car you want is important—and electric cars might not be the right choice for everyone.

Know the Facts!

The earliest electric **vehicle** (EV) was invented in the 1830s. In 1890, an EV was built in the United States that could travel at speeds of up to 14 miles (22.5 km) per hour, which was fast for its time!

early electric vehicle

You may not need to buy a car yet, but the **debate** about electric cars is sure to continue for a long time. Before you decide how you feel about these vehicles, it's important to learn the facts!

San Diego Convention Ctr
NEXT EXIT
GASLAMP QUARTER

Under the
HOOD

How do electric cars work? They're powered by a large **battery** pack. This battery pack needs to be charged the same way the battery in a smartphone or tablet needs to be charged. This is done by plugging it into an outlet in a wall or by using another kind of charging **equipment**, like what can be found at a charging station.

This is very different from how a car that uses gasoline works. A gas-powered car has an internal combustion engine. With this kind of engine, air and gasoline are set on fire by a spark, and that powers the car.

Know the Facts!

Another kind of car uses both an internal combustion engine and a battery. This is called a hybrid vehicle.

gas-powered car

Electric cars and gas-powered cars may look alike in many ways, but what goes on under the hood is very different!

electric car

GASES

Cars that use gasoline produce emissions. This means they put gases known as greenhouse gases into the air. Greenhouse gases trap heat from the sun in Earth's **atmosphere**, which makes Earth warmer. This has led to climate change, which is a change in weather patterns on Earth over time.

Electric cars don't produce these kinds of emissions. Driving them causes less air pollution than driving gas-powered cars. Many people believe switching to electric cars can play a big part in slowing or even stopping climate change.

Know the Facts!

One of the main greenhouse gases emitted, or put into the air, from gas-powered cars is carbon dioxide. A **typical** car in the United States that runs on gasoline emits 5 tons (4.6 metric tons) of carbon dioxide every year!

OZONE LAYER

GREENHOUSE GASES

Emissions from gas-powered cars come out of their tailpipe, which is shown here. Electric cars produce no tailpipe emissions. These emissions play a part in what's known as the greenhouse effect, which is making Earth get warmer faster than it would naturally.

MONEY

Many people believe electric cars are better for the environment than cars that use gasoline. This had led to an increase in the number of people buying electric cars around the world. However, most Americans are still buying gas-powered cars. One of the biggest reasons for this is price.

Generally, electric cars cost much more to buy than cars that use gasoline. Many families don't have the money to own such an expensive car. It also costs money to set up a charging station for an electric car in the owner's home. This makes the total cost even higher.

Know the Facts!

As of 2022, around 1 percent of all the cars in the United States were electric.

Not everyone can afford an electric car. Many Americans
have to work hard and save up for a long time to buy any car,
so finding something affordable is more important than anything else.

Surprise
SAVINGS

It generally costs more to buy an electric car than a gas-powered one. However, some people argue that electric cars save their owners money over time. They have fewer moving parts than gas-powered cars. This can make electric cars cheaper to maintain, or to keep working.

People also argue that it costs less money to keep charging an electric car than it does to keep filling a car with gasoline. A 2020 study showed that people who owned electric cars spent 60 percent less to power their car each year than people who owned gas-powered cars.

Know the Facts!

The U.S. government offers tax credits, or money that's taken off what's owed in taxes, for owning an electric car. This tax credit can save people up to $7,500!

Although charging an electric car at home
can raise electricity costs, studies have shown it's often
still cheaper over time than filling a car with gasoline.

Problems with
CHARGING

It may cost less in the long run to charge an electric car, but it can be hard to find a charging station on the road. There are far fewer EV charging stations than there are gas stations in the United States as of 2023. This can make it much harder to take an electric car on a long road trip than a gas-powered car.

In addition, it takes much longer to charge an electric car than it does to fill a car with gas. It can take hours to charge an electric car—and sometimes even days!

Know the Facts!

The fastest charging systems available as of 2023 take between 30 and 45 minutes to charge an electric car to 80 percent.

Some office buildings, hotels, and other places where people stay for a long time have EV charging stations. This is because it can take many hours for an electric car to charge, especially if the weather is cold.

Many EV drivers only need to charge their car at home. This saves time because they never need to stop for gas. Instead, they can plug their car in at night, and in many cases, it'll be charged by morning.

Most electric cars can meet the daily travel needs of their drivers without needing to be charged more than once a day. The average American driver travels less than 100 miles (161 km) each day, and most electric cars can travel more than 200 miles (322 km) with a fully-charged battery.

Know the Facts!

In 2021, it was reported that 80 percent of all EV charging was done at home.

16

People who support the use of electric cars often point out the ease of charging at home instead of going to a gas station. EV owners also don't have to worry as much about the price of gas, which can go up because of world events, changes in taxes, and many other reasons.

Fewer CHOICES

Many people spend a lot of time in their cars. Because of this, they want to buy exactly the kind of car that best meets their needs. This isn't always easy if they only want to look at electric cars.

There are far fewer kinds of electric cars than gas-powered cars. Some people don't like the idea of having fewer choices when it comes to the kind of car they buy. They believe everyone should get to choose the right car for them—and that includes being able to choose either a gas-powered car or an electric one.

Know the Facts!

The biggest name in EVs is Tesla. The only cars this company makes are electric cars, and it's been a leader in the EV business since 2008, when it came out with its first all-electric car, the Roadster.

Tesla Roadster

Having the freedom to choose any kind of car is very important for some people.

TOGETHER

As climate change continues to cause more problems for all of us living on Earth, people are looking for ways to help. Driving electric cars has become one way people are trying to lower the amount of greenhouse gases they put into the air. However, greenhouse gases are often emitted during the **process** of generating the electricity needed to charge electric cars. Also, mining for the **materials** to make EV batteries can cause some harm to the environment.

After learning all the facts, do you think everyone should drive electric cars? Which facts would you use to support your argument?

Know the Facts!

Greenhouse gases are put into the air when coal, oil, or natural gas are burned to generate, or produce, electricity. Using wind, water, or the sun to generate electricity is greener—better for the environment.

Should everyone drive electric cars?

YES

- Electric cars produce fewer emissions, which can help fight climate change.

- Charging electric cars costs less money in the long run than filling a car with gasoline.

- Electric cars cost less money to maintain.

- Most people can charge an electric car at home instead of taking a trip to the gas station, which saves time.

NO

- Electric cars are more expensive than other cars, and not everyone can afford them.

- There are fewer charging stations than gas stations, and it can take a long time to charge an electric car.

- People should be able to choose exactly what kind of car they want to drive.

- Generating the electricity needed to charge electric cars and mining to make the batteries can harm the environment.

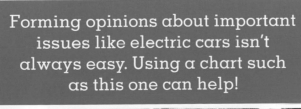

Forming opinions about important issues like electric cars isn't always easy. Using a chart such as this one can help!

GLOSSARY

atmosphere: The whole mass of air surrounding Earth.

battery: An electric cell or connected electric cells that provide power for a machine.

debate: An argument or discussion about an issue, generally between two sides.

equipment: Supplies or tools needed for a certain purpose.

material: Something from which something else can be made.

process: A set of actions.

typical: Showing the essential characteristics of a group.

vehicle: A machine used to carry people and goods from one place to another.

For More INFORMATION

WEBSITES

Electric Vehicle Charging Station Locations
afdc.energy.gov/fuels/electricity_locations.html#/find/nearest?fuel=ELEC
Visitors to this website can search on a map for the locations of EV charging stations across the United States.

NASA ClimateKids: "What Is the Greenhouse Effect?"
climatekids.nasa.gov/greenhouse-effect/
This website explains why greenhouse gases are such a big problem.

BOOKS

Dickmann, Nancy. *Electric Cars*. North Mankato, MN: Capstone Press, 2021.

Eschbach, Christina. *Inside Electric Cars*. Minneapolis, MN: Core Library, 2019.

Heitkamp, Kristina Lyn. *Electric Cars*. Lake Elmo, MN: Focus Readers, 2022.

INDEX